To:

_____

From:

_____

Date:

_____

Delight yourself in the LORD, and He will
give you the desires of your heart. PS. 37:4

The LORD is my light and my salvation—whom shall I fear? The LORD is the stronghold of my life—of whom shall I be afraid? PS. 27:1

The Lord Himself goes before you and
will be with you; He will never leave you
nor forsake you. DEUT. 31:8

God is working in you, giving you the
desire to obey Him and the power to do
what pleases Him. PHIL. 2:13

I can do everything through Christ,
who gives me strength. PHIL. 4:13

If you want to know what God wants you to do,
ask Him, and He will gladly tell you. JAMES 1:5

Create in me a pure heart, O God, and renew
a steadfast spirit within me. PS. 51:10

If anyone is in Christ, he is a new creation; the old has gone, the new has come! 2 COR. 5:17

Cast your cares on the LORD and He
will sustain you. PS. 55:22

The LORD your God is with you, He is mighty to save. He will take great delight in you, He will quiet you with His love. ZEPH. 3:17

The LORD is faithful to all His promises
and loving toward all He has made. PS. 145:13

In You, O Lord, do I put my trust.
PS. 71:1

"Be strong and courageous … the LORD your God
will be with you wherever you go." JOSH. 1:9

Depend on the LORD in whatever you do,
and your plans will succeed. PROV. 16:3

Since we have been justified through
faith, we have peace with God through
our Lord Jesus Christ. ROM. 5:1

The Lord is my rock, my fortress and my deliverer;
my God is my rock, in Whom I take refuge. PS. 18:2

"If anyone would come after Me, he must deny himself and take up his cross and follow Me." MATT. 16:24

The word of the LORD is right and true;
He is faithful in all He does. PS. 33:4

The LORD is my strength, my shield from every danger.
I trust in Him with all my heart. PS. 28:7

In Him we have redemption through His blood, the forgiveness of sins, in accordance with the riches of God's grace. EPH. 1:7

I trust in Your unfailing love. I will rejoice
because You have rescued me. PS. 13:5

Live a life of love, just as Christ loved us
and gave Himself up for us. EPH. 5:2

_____

_____

_____

_____

_____

_____

_____

_____

_____

_____

_____

_____

_____

_____

_____

_____

_____

_____

_____

_____

_____

_____

_____

"You will seek Me and find Me when you seek
Me with all your heart." JER. 29:13

My soul finds rest in God alone;
my salvation comes from Him. PS. 62:1

Delight yourself in the LORD, and He will
give you the desires of your heart. PS. 37:4

The LORD is my light and my salvation—whom shall I fear? The LORD is the stronghold of my life—of whom shall I be afraid? PS. 27:1

The LORD Himself goes before you and
will be with you; He will never leave you
nor forsake you. DEUT. 31:8

God is working in you, giving you the
desire to obey Him and the power to do
what pleases Him. PHIL. 2:13

I can do everything through Christ,
who gives me strength. PHIL. 4:13

If you want to know what God wants you to do,
ask Him, and He will gladly tell you. JAMES 1:5

_____

_____

_____

_____

_____

_____

_____

_____

_____

_____

_____

_____

_____

_____

_____

_____

_____

_____

_____

_____

_____

Create in me a pure heart, O God, and renew
a steadfast spirit within me. PS. 51:10

If anyone is in Christ, he is a new creation;
the old has gone, the new has come! 2 COR. 5:17

Cast your cares on the LORD and He
will sustain you. PS. 55:22

The LORD your God is with you, He is mighty to save. He will take great delight in you, He will quiet you with His love. ZEPH. 3:17

The LORD is faithful to all His promises
and loving toward all He has made. PS. 145:13

In You, O Lᴏʀᴅ, do I put my trust.

"Be strong and courageous ... the LORD your God will be with you wherever you go." JOSH. 1:9

Depend on the LORD in whatever you do,
and your plans will succeed. PROV. 16:3

Since we have been justified through
faith, we have peace with God through
our Lord Jesus Christ. ROM. 5:1

The LORD is my rock, my fortress and my deliverer; my God is my rock, in Whom I take refuge. PS. 18:2

"If anyone would come after Me, he must deny himself and take up his cross and follow Me." MATT. 16:24

The word of the Lord is right and true;
He is faithful in all He does. PS. 33:4

The LORD is my strength, my shield from every danger.
I trust in Him with all my heart. PS. 28:7

In Him we have redemption through His blood,
the forgiveness of sins, in accordance with the
riches of God's grace. EPH. 1:7

I trust in Your unfailing love. I will rejoice
because You have rescued me. PS. 13:5

Live a life of love, just as Christ loved us
and gave Himself up for us. EPH. 5:2

"You will seek Me and find Me when you seek
Me with all your heart." JER. 29:13

My soul finds rest in God alone;
my salvation comes from Him. PS. 62:1

Delight yourself in the LORD, and He will
give you the desires of your heart. PS. 37:4

The LORD is my light and my salvation—whom shall I fear? The LORD is the stronghold of my life— of whom shall I be afraid? PS. 27:1

The LORD Himself goes before you and
will be with you; He will never leave you
nor forsake you. DEUT. 31:8

God is working in you, giving you the
desire to obey Him and the power to do
what pleases Him. PHIL. 2:13

I can do everything through Christ,
who gives me strength. PHIL. 4:13

If you want to know what God wants you to do, ask Him, and He will gladly tell you. JAMES 1:5

Create in me a pure heart, O God, and renew
a steadfast spirit within me. PS. 51:10

If anyone is in Christ, he is a new creation;
the old has gone, the new has come! 2 COR. 5:17

Cast your cares on the Lord and He
will sustain you. PS. 55:22

The LORD your God is with you, He is mighty to save. He will take great delight in you, He will quiet you with His love. ZEPH. 3:17

The LORD is faithful to all His promises
and loving toward all He has made. PS. 145:13

In You, O LORD, do I put my trust.

PS. 71:1

"Be strong and courageous ... the LORD your God
will be with you wherever you go." JOSH. 1:9

Depend on the LORD in whatever you do,
and your plans will succeed. PROV. 16:3

Since we have been justified through faith, we have peace with God through our Lord Jesus Christ. ROM. 5:1

The LORD is my rock, my fortress and my deliverer; my God is my rock, in Whom I take refuge. PS. 18:2

"If anyone would come after Me, he must deny himself and take up his cross and follow Me." MATT. 16:24

The word of the LORD is right and true;
He is faithful in all He does. PS. 33:4

The Lord is my strength, my shield from every danger.
I trust in Him with all my heart. PS. 28:7

In Him we have redemption through His blood, the forgiveness of sins, in accordance with the riches of God's grace. EPH. 1:7

I trust in Your unfailing love. I will rejoice
because You have rescued me. PS. 13:5

Live a life of love, just as Christ loved us
and gave Himself up for us. EPH. 5:2

"You will seek Me and find Me when you seek Me with all your heart." JER. 29:13

My soul finds rest in God alone;
my salvation comes from Him. PS. 62:1

Delight yourself in the LORD, and He will give you the desires of your heart. PS. 37:4

The LORD is my light and my salvation—whom shall I fear? The LORD is the stronghold of my life—of whom shall I be afraid? PS. 27:1

The Lord Himself goes before you and
will be with you; He will never leave you
nor forsake you. DEUT. 31:8

God is working in you, giving you the
desire to obey Him and the power to do
what pleases Him. PHIL. 2:13

I can do everything through Christ,
who gives me strength. PHIL. 4:13

If you want to know what God wants you to do,
ask Him, and He will gladly tell you. JAMES 1:5

Create in me a pure heart, O God, and renew
a steadfast spirit within me. PS. 51:10

If anyone is in Christ, he is a new creation;
the old has gone, the new has come! 2 COR. 5:17

Cast your cares on the LORD and He
will sustain you. PS. 55:22

The LORD your God is with you, He is mighty to save. He will take great delight in you, He will quiet you with His love. ZEPH. 3:17

The LORD is faithful to all His promises
and loving toward all He has made. PS. 145:13

In You, O Lᴏʀᴅ, do I put my trust.

PS. 71:1

"Be strong and courageous ... the LORD your God will be with you wherever you go." JOSH. 1:9

Depend on the Lᴏʀᴅ in whatever you do,
and your plans will succeed. PROV. 16:3

Since we have been justified through
faith, we have peace with God through
our Lord Jesus Christ. ROM. 5:1

The Lord is my rock, my fortress and my deliverer;
my God is my rock, in Whom I take refuge. PS. 18:2

"If anyone would come after Me, he must deny himself and take up his cross and follow Me." MATT. 16:24

The word of the LORD is right and true;
He is faithful in all He does. PS. 33:4

The LORD is my strength, my shield from every danger.
I trust in Him with all my heart. PS. 28:7

In Him we have redemption through His blood, the forgiveness of sins, in accordance with the riches of God's grace. EPH. 1:7

I trust in Your unfailing love. I will rejoice
because You have rescued me. PS. 13:5

Live a life of love, just as Christ loved us
and gave Himself up for us. EPH. 5:2

"You will seek Me and find Me when you seek Me with all your heart." JER. 29:13

My soul finds rest in God alone;
my salvation comes from Him. PS. 62:1

Delight yourself in the Lord, and He will
give you the desires of your heart. PS. 37:4

The LORD is my light and my salvation—whom shall I fear? The LORD is the stronghold of my life—of whom shall I be afraid? PS. 27:1

The LORD Himself goes before you and
will be with you; He will never leave you
nor forsake you. DEUT. 31:8

God is working in you, giving you the
desire to obey Him and the power to do
what pleases Him. PHIL. 2:13

I can do everything through Christ,
who gives me strength. PHIL. 4:13

If you want to know what God wants you to do,
ask Him, and He will gladly tell you. JAMES 1:5

Create in me a pure heart, O God, and renew
a steadfast spirit within me. PS. 51:10

If anyone is in Christ, he is a new creation; the old has gone, the new has come! 2 COR. 5:17

Cast your cares on the LORD and He
will sustain you. PS. 55:22

The LORD your God is with you, He is mighty to save. He will take great delight in you, He will quiet you with His love. ZEPH. 3:17

The LORD is faithful to all His promises
and loving toward all He has made. PS. 145:13

In You, O LORD, do I put my trust.

PS. 71:1

"Be strong and courageous ... the LORD your God
will be with you wherever you go." JOSH. 1:9

Depend on the LORD in whatever you do,
and your plans will succeed. PROV. 16:3

Since we have been justified through
faith, we have peace with God through
our Lord Jesus Christ. ROM. 5:1

The Lord is my rock, my fortress and my deliverer;
my God is my rock, in Whom I take refuge. PS. 18:2

"If anyone would come after Me, he must deny himself and take up his cross and follow Me." MATT. 16:24

The word of the LORD is right and true;
He is faithful in all He does. PS. 33:4

The LORD is my strength, my shield from every danger.
I trust in Him with all my heart. PS. 28:7

In Him we have redemption through His blood, the forgiveness of sins, in accordance with the riches of God's grace. EPH. 1:7

I trust in Your unfailing love. I will rejoice
because You have rescued me. PS. 13:5

Live a life of love, just as Christ loved us
and gave Himself up for us. EPH. 5:2

"You will seek Me and find Me when you seek Me with all your heart." JER. 29:13

My soul finds rest in God alone;
my salvation comes from Him. PS. 62:1

Delight yourself in the LORD, and He will
give you the desires of your heart. PS. 37:4

The LORD is my light and my salvation—whom shall I fear? The LORD is the stronghold of my life—of whom shall I be afraid? PS. 27:1

The LORD Himself goes before you and will be with you; He will never leave you nor forsake you. DEUT. 31:8

God is working in you, giving you the
desire to obey Him and the power to do
what pleases Him. PHIL. 2:13

I can do everything through Christ,
who gives me strength. PHIL. 4:13

If you want to know what God wants you to do,
ask Him, and He will gladly tell you. JAMES 1:5

Create in me a pure heart, O God, and renew
a steadfast spirit within me. PS. 51:10

If anyone is in Christ, he is a new creation;
the old has gone, the new has come! 2 COR. 5:17

Cast your cares on the LORD and He
will sustain you. PS. 55:22

The LORD your God is with you, He is mighty to save. He will take great delight in you, He will quiet you with His love. ZEPH. 3:17

The LORD is faithful to all His promises
and loving toward all He has made. PS. 145:13

In You, O LORD, do I put my trust.

PS. 71:1

"Be strong and courageous ... the LORD your God
will be with you wherever you go." JOSH. 1:9

Depend on the LORD in whatever you do,
and your plans will succeed. PROV. 16:3

Since we have been justified through
faith, we have peace with God through
our Lord Jesus Christ. ROM. 5:1

The Lord is my rock, my fortress and my deliverer;
my God is my rock, in Whom I take refuge. PS. 18:2

"If anyone would come after Me, he must deny himself and take up his cross and follow Me." MATT. 16:24

The word of the LORD is right and true;
He is faithful in all He does. PS. 33:4

The LORD is my strength, my shield from every danger.
I trust in Him with all my heart. PS. 28:7

In Him we have redemption through His blood,
the forgiveness of sins, in accordance with the
riches of God's grace. EPH. 1:7

I trust in Your unfailing love. I will rejoice
because You have rescued me. PS. 13:5

Live a life of love, just as Christ loved us
and gave Himself up for us. EPH. 5:2

"You will seek Me and find Me when you seek
Me with all your heart." JER. 29:13

My soul finds rest in God alone;
my salvation comes from Him. PS. 62:1

Delight yourself in the LORD, and He will
give you the desires of your heart. PS. 37:4

The LORD is my light and my salvation—whom shall I fear? The LORD is the stronghold of my life—of whom shall I be afraid? PS. 27:1

The LORD Himself goes before you and
will be with you; He will never leave you
nor forsake you. DEUT. 31:8

God is working in you, giving you the
desire to obey Him and the power to do
what pleases Him. PHIL. 2:13

I can do everything through Christ,
who gives me strength. PHIL. 4:13

If you want to know what God wants you to do,
ask Him, and He will gladly tell you. JAMES 1:5

Create in me a pure heart, O God, and renew
a steadfast spirit within me. PS. 51:10

If anyone is in Christ, he is a new creation;
the old has gone, the new has come! 2 COR. 5:17

Cast your cares on the LORD and He
will sustain you. PS. 55:22

The LORD your God is with you, He is mighty to save. He will take great delight in you, He will quiet you with His love. ZEPH. 3:17

The Lord is faithful to all His promises
and loving toward all He has made. PS. 145:13

In You, O Lord, do I put my trust.

PS. 71:1

"Be strong and courageous ... the LORD your God will be with you wherever you go." JOSH. 1:9

Depend on the LORD in whatever you do,
and your plans will succeed. PROV. 16:3

Since we have been justified through
faith, we have peace with God through
our Lord Jesus Christ. ROM. 5:1

The LORD is my rock, my fortress and my deliverer;
my God is my rock, in Whom I take refuge. PS. 18:2

"If anyone would come after Me, he must deny himself and take up his cross and follow Me." MATT. 16:24

The word of the LORD is right and true;
He is faithful in all He does. PS. 33:4

The LORD is my strength, my shield from every danger.
I trust in Him with all my heart. PS. 28:7

In Him we have redemption through His blood,
the forgiveness of sins, in accordance with the
riches of God's grace. EPH. 1:7

I trust in Your unfailing love. I will rejoice
because You have rescued me. PS. 13:5

Live a life of love, just as Christ loved us
and gave Himself up for us. EPH. 5:2

"You will seek Me and find Me when you seek
Me with all your heart." JER. 29:13

My soul finds rest in God alone;
my salvation comes from Him. PS. 62:1

Delight yourself in the LORD, and He will give you the desires of your heart. PS. 37:4

The LORD is my light and my salvation—whom shall I fear? The LORD is the stronghold of my life—of whom shall I be afraid? PS. 27:1

The LORD Himself goes before you and
will be with you; He will never leave you
nor forsake you. DEUT. 31:8

God is working in you, giving you the
desire to obey Him and the power to do
what pleases Him. PHIL. 2:13

I can do everything through Christ,
who gives me strength. PHIL. 4:13

If you want to know what God wants you to do,
ask Him, and He will gladly tell you. JAMES 1:5

Create in me a pure heart, O God, and renew
a steadfast spirit within me. PS. 51:10

If anyone is in Christ, he is a new creation;
the old has gone, the new has come! 2 COR. 5:17

Cast your cares on the LORD and He
will sustain you. PS. 55:22

The Lord your God is with you, He is mighty to save. He will take great delight in you, He will quiet you with His love. ZEPH. 3:17

The LORD is faithful to all His promises
and loving toward all He has made. PS. 145:13

In You, O LORD, do I put my trust.
PS. 71:1

"Be strong and courageous ... the LORD your God will be with you wherever you go." JOSH. 1:9

Depend on the LORD in whatever you do,
and your plans will succeed. PROV. 16:3

Since we have been justified through
faith, we have peace with God through
our Lord Jesus Christ. ROM. 5:1

The LORD is my rock, my fortress and my deliverer;
my God is my rock, in Whom I take refuge. PS. 18:2

"If anyone would come after Me, he must deny himself and take up his cross and follow Me." MATT. 16:24

The word of the LORD is right and true;
He is faithful in all He does. PS. 33:4

The LORD is my strength, my shield from every danger.
I trust in Him with all my heart. PS. 28:7

In Him we have redemption through His blood, the forgiveness of sins, in accordance with the riches of God's grace. EPH. 1:7

_____

_____

_____

_____

_____

_____

_____

_____

_____

_____

_____

_____

_____

_____

_____

_____

_____

_____

_____

_____

_____

_____

I trust in Your unfailing love. I will rejoice
because You have rescued me. PS. 13:5

Live a life of love, just as Christ loved us
and gave Himself up for us. EPH. 5:2

"You will seek Me and find Me when you seek
Me with all your heart." JER. 29:13

My soul finds rest in God alone;
my salvation comes from Him. PS. 62:1

Delight yourself in the LORD, and He will give you the desires of your heart. PS. 37:4

The LORD is my light and my salvation—whom
shall I fear? The LORD is the stronghold of my life—
of whom shall I be afraid? PS. 27:1

The LORD Himself goes before you and
will be with you; He will never leave you
nor forsake you. DEUT. 31:8

God is working in you, giving you the
desire to obey Him and the power to do
what pleases Him. PHIL. 2:13

I can do everything through Christ,
who gives me strength. PHIL. 4:13

If you want to know what God wants you to do,
ask Him, and He will gladly tell you. JAMES 1:5

Create in me a pure heart, O God, and renew
a steadfast spirit within me. PS. 51:10

If anyone is in Christ, he is a new creation;
the old has gone, the new has come! 2 COR. 5:17

Cast your cares on the LORD and He
will sustain you. PS. 55:22

The LORD your God is with you, He is mighty to save. He will take great delight in you, He will quiet you with His love. ZEPH. 3:17

The LORD is faithful to all His promises
and loving toward all He has made. PS. 145:13

In You, O LORD, do I put my trust.

PS. 71:1

"Be strong and courageous ... the LORD your God
will be with you wherever you go." JOSH. 1:9

Depend on the Lord in whatever you do,
and your plans will succeed. PROV. 16:3

Since we have been justified through
faith, we have peace with God through
our Lord Jesus Christ. ROM. 5:1

The LORD is my rock, my fortress and my deliverer;
my God is my rock, in Whom I take refuge. PS. 18:2

"If anyone would come after Me, he must deny himself and take up his cross and follow Me." MATT. 16:24

The word of the LORD is right and true;
He is faithful in all He does. PS. 33:4

The LORD is my strength, my shield from every danger.
I trust in Him with all my heart. PS. 28:7

In Him we have redemption through His blood,
the forgiveness of sins, in accordance with the
riches of God's grace. EPH. 1:7

I trust in Your unfailing love. I will rejoice
because You have rescued me. PS. 13:5

Live a life of love, just as Christ loved us
and gave Himself up for us. EPH. 5:2

"You will seek Me and find Me when you seek
Me with all your heart." JER. 29:13

My soul finds rest in God alone;
my salvation comes from Him. PS. 62:1